WUNDERKEYS INTER[MEDIATE]

POP STUDIES FOR PIANO 1

A Pop-Infused Lesson Companion To Reinforce
Scales, Chords, Triads, And Left-Hand Patterns

WunderKeys Intermediate Pop Studies For Piano 1 by Andrea and Trevor Dow
Copyright © 2019 Teach Music Today Learning Solutions
www.teachpianotoday.com and www.wunderkeys.com

WunderKeys Intermediate Pop Studies For Piano 1 is jam-packed with pop-infused piano studies. Get ready for a cool workout in the keys of C Major, A Minor, G Major, E Minor, F Major, and D Minor as you turn technical exercises into powerful pop music.

TABLE OF CONTENTS

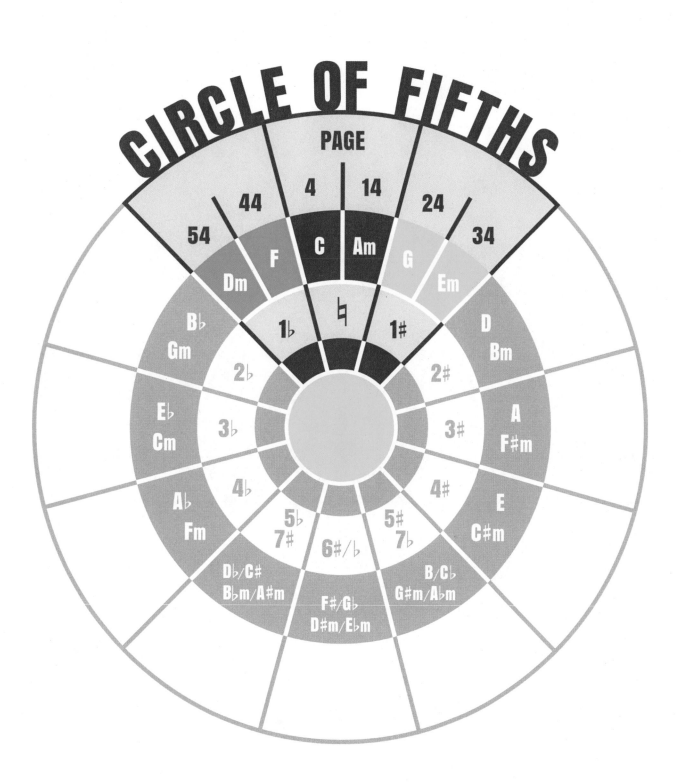

CIRCLE OF FIFTHS

C MAJOR
C MAJOR

It's time to power up your piano skills in the key of C major with pop-infused scale practice, lead sheet triad training, chord crunching, and left-hand pattern improv. **Let's get started!**

C MAJOR MAP

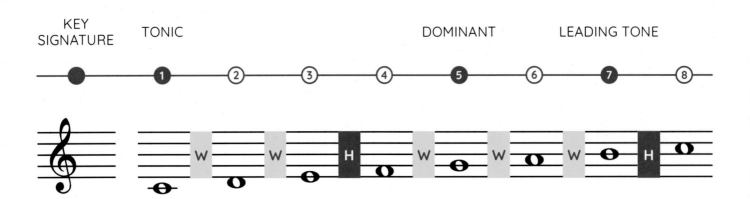

POP PIANO CHORDS

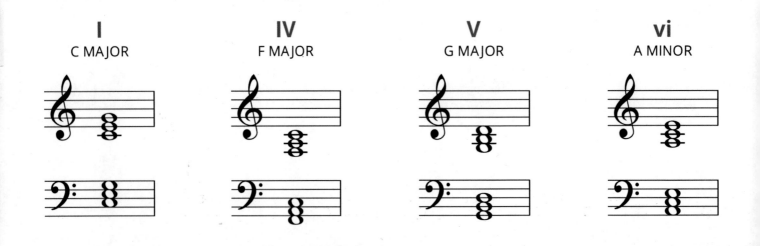

I	IV	V	vi
C MAJOR	F MAJOR	G MAJOR	A MINOR

C MAJOR
SCALE PRACTICE

C MAJOR SCALE

Practice playing a two-octave C major scale using the fingering patterns on the keyboard images and the notes on the grand staff.

LH Pattern

RH Pattern

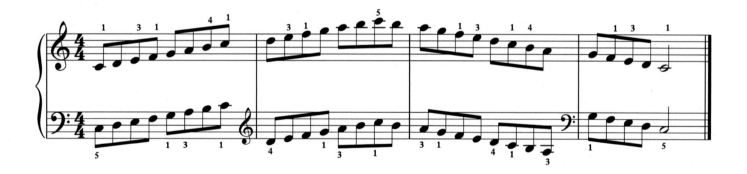

CONTRARY MOTION

Practice playing a two-octave C major scale in contrary motion. When you are ready, play the scale-focused pop piano piece on the following page.

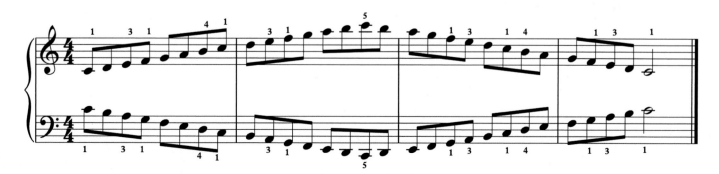

DREAMER
A C MAJOR SCALE STUDY

With Expression

DREAMER
A C MAJOR SCALE STUDY

LEAD SHEET
TRIAD TRAINING

Let's put some pop in your triad training with lead sheets. **A lead sheet** uses chord symbols above the treble staff in place of the bass staff. Chord symbols dictate which chords your left hand plays while accompanying your right hand.

LET'S GET STARTED

1 The C major triad consists of the I chord (root) and its first and second inversions. Let's practice playing the triad of C major. We'll begin with a solid triad.

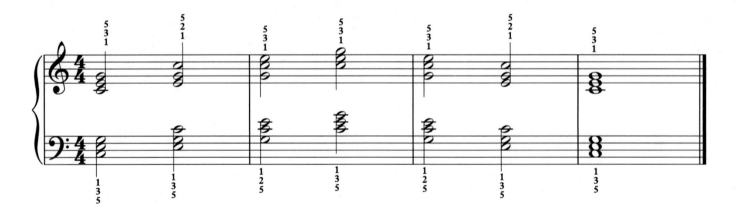

▶ Now let's practice playing the broken triad of C major. When playing a broken triad your tone should be smooth and even. Be careful not to accent the first note of each broken inversion.

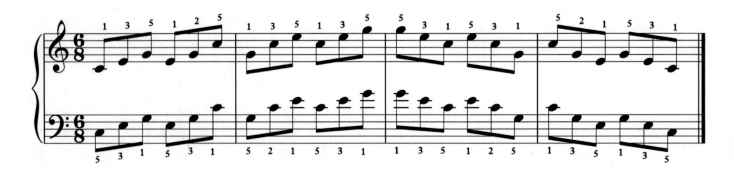

2 Next, let's learn how to play from a lead sheet. A lead sheet looks like this:

▶ When practicing the line of music above, you can play the chords as held fifths, like this:

3 Finally, play the lead sheet below to rock the C major triad.

SIGHT READING
POP PIANO CHORDS

Look at the **primary chords** of C major in the measures of music below. Can you find a I chord? Can you find a IV chord? Can you find a V chord? Can you find a vi chord?

PICK A PATH

Beginning at the purple box and ending at the yellow box, play the four measures of music that rest on the dotted path. Next, I will use a colored crayon to draw a new four-measure path that begins at the purple box and ends at the yellow box. Try playing along the new path. **Let's play again.**

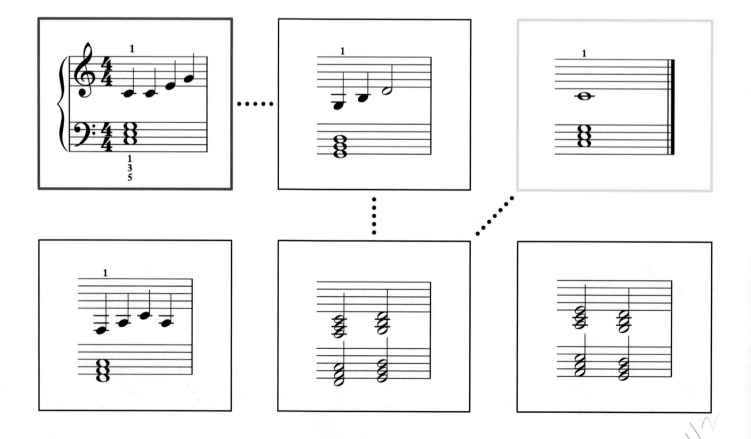

RHYTHM ROCK
POP PIANO CHORDS

Let's reinforce the primary chords of C major with a Lap Tap Clap Rhythm Duet. First, practice the body percussion above the grand staff below. Stem-down notes are performed by tapping both hands on your lap. Stem-up notes are performed by clapping your hands together. X note heads are performed by tapping your knuckles on a hard surface. Next, I will play the music as an accompaniment while you perform the body percussion. Finally, let's switch roles.

LAP TAP CLAP DUET

POP IMPROV
LEFT-HAND PATTERNS

Let's combine **left-hand patterns** with improvisation to create a pop-worthy piano experience. To begin, practice the left-hand pattern below on each of the primary chords of C major. Then, when you are ready, use any combination of notes from the C major five-finger scale to show off your improv skills on the piece that follows this page.

LET'S GET STARTED

1 First, practice playing broken 5ths on the primary chords below.

C (I)   F (IV)   G (V)   Am (vi)

2 Using any combination of notes from the C major five-finger scale, practice improvising a melody to match the provided rhythm as you play the left-hand chord progression below.

SEVENTEEN
A POP PATTERN STUDY

Let's try again! As you play this piece, use any combination of notes from the
C major five-finger scale to improvise a melody that matches the provided rhythm.

A MINOR
A MINOR

It's time to power up your piano skills in the key of A minor with pop-infused scale practice, lead sheet triad training, chord crunching, and left-hand pattern improv. **Let's get started!**

A MINOR MAP

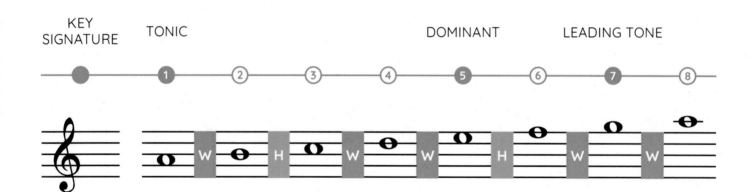

KEY SIGNATURE	TONIC				DOMINANT		LEADING TONE	
	1	2	3	4	5	6	7	8

POP PIANO CHORDS

i
A MINOR

iv
D MINOR

v
E MINOR

VI
F MAJOR

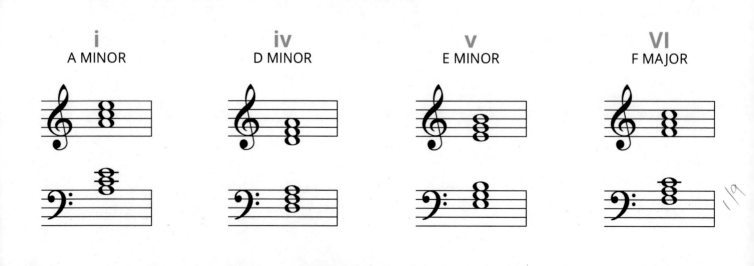

A MINOR SCALE PRACTICE

A NATURAL MINOR SCALE

Practice playing a two-octave A natural minor scale using the fingering patterns on the keyboard images and the notes on the grand staff.

LH Pattern

RH Pattern

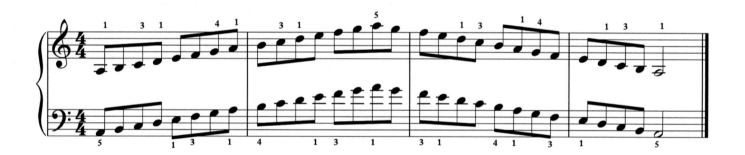

A HARMONIC MINOR SCALE

When playing the A harmonic minor scale, the leading tone (7th) is raised a half step. This is indicated by the colored notes on the staff below. Practice playing the scale.

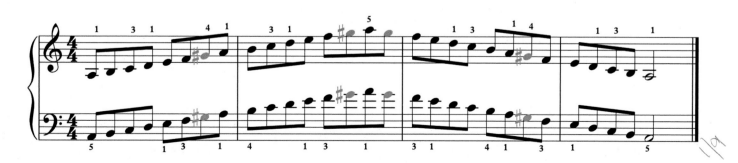

LABYRINTH
AN A MINOR SCALE STUDY

Brooding

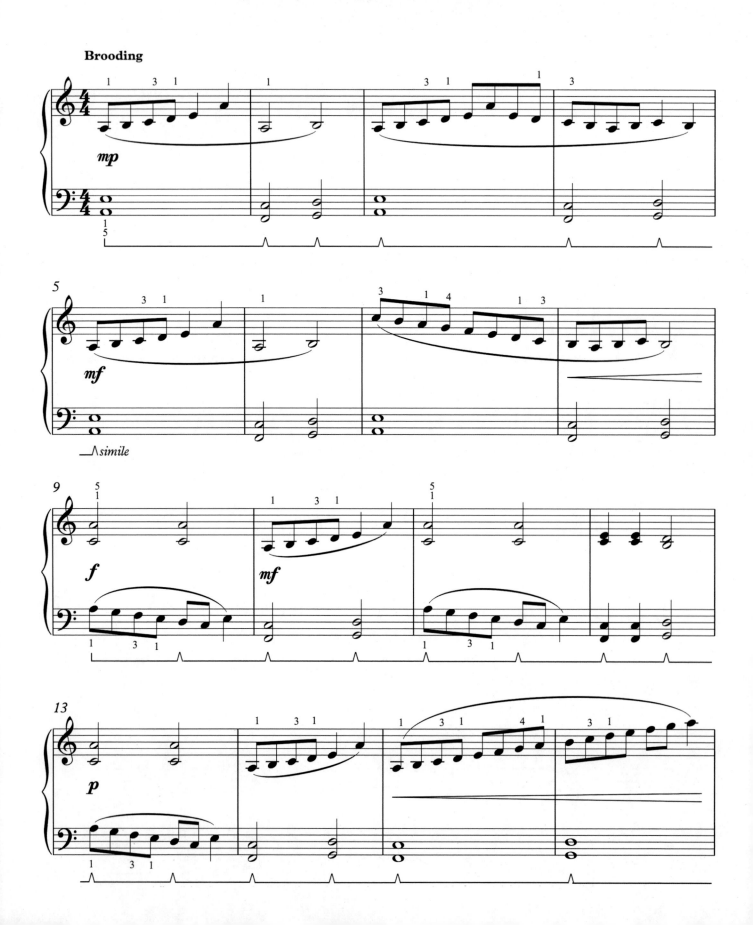

LABYRINTH
AN A MINOR SCALE STUDY

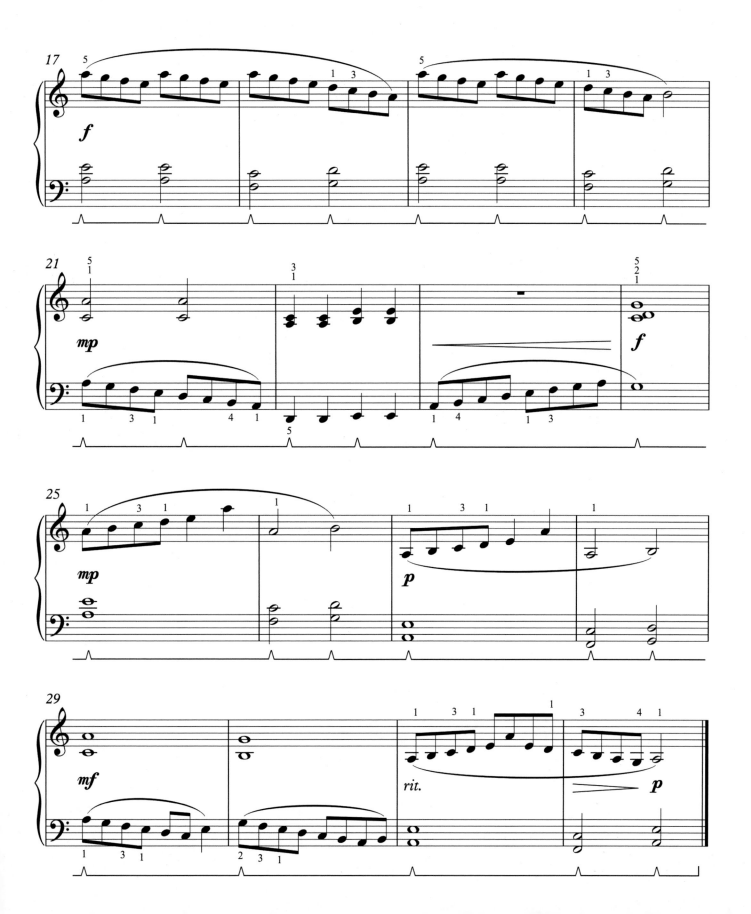

LEAD SHEET
TRIAD TRAINING

Let's put some pop in your triad training with lead sheets. **A lead sheet** uses chord symbols above the treble staff in place of the bass staff. Chord symbols dictate which chords your left hand plays while accompanying your right hand.

LET'S GET STARTED

1 The A minor triad consists of the i chord (root) and its first and second inversions. Let's practice playing the triad of A minor. We'll begin with a solid triad.

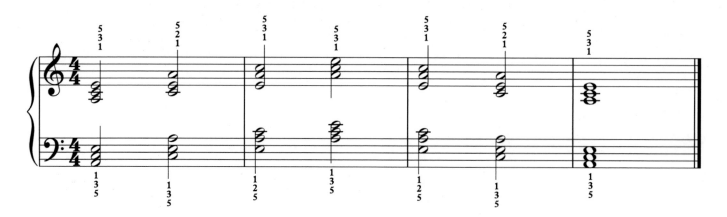

▶ Now let's practice playing the broken triad of A minor. When playing a broken triad your tone should be smooth and even. Be careful not to accent the first note of each broken inversion.

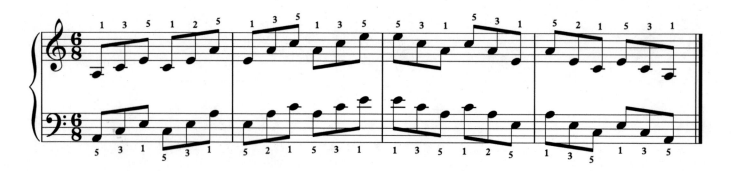

2 Next, let's learn how to play from a lead sheet. A lead sheet looks like this:

▶ When practicing the line of music above, you can play the chords as held fifths, like this:

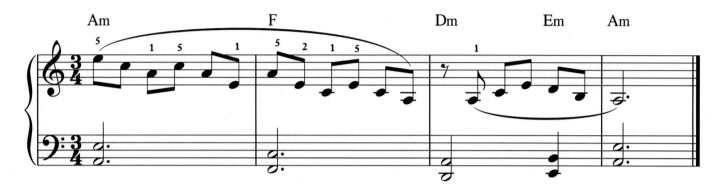

3 Finally, play the lead sheet below to rock the A minor triad.

SIGHT READING
POP PIANO CHORDS

Look at the **primary chords** of A minor in the measures of music below. Can you find a i chord? Can you find a iv chord? Can you find a v chord? Can you find a VI chord?

PICK A PATH

Beginning at the green box and ending at the pink box, play the four measures of music that rest on the dotted path. Next, I will use a colored crayon to draw a new four-measure path that begins at the green box and ends at the pink box. Try playing along the new path. **Let's play again.**

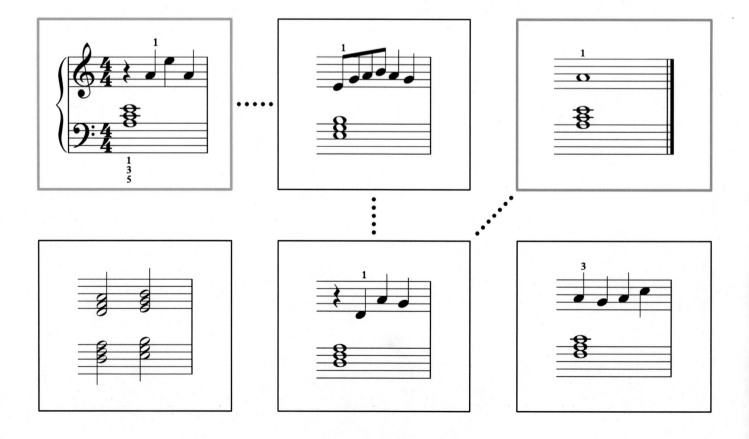

RHYTHM ROCK
POP PIANO CHORDS

Let's reinforce the primary chords of A minor with a Lap Tap Clap Rhythm Duet. First, practice the body percussion above the grand staff below. Stem-down notes are performed by tapping both hands on your lap. Stem-up notes are performed by clapping your hands together. X note heads are performed by tapping your knuckles on a hard surface. Next, I will play the music as an accompaniment while you perform the body percussion. Finally, let's switch roles.

LAP TAP CLAP DUET

POP IMPROV
LEFT-HAND PATTERNS

Let's combine **left-hand patterns** with improvisation to create a pop-worthy piano experience. To begin, practice the left-hand pattern below on each of the primary chords of A minor. Then, when you are ready, use any combination of notes from the A minor five-finger scale to show off your improv skills on the piece that follows this page.

LET'S GET STARTED

1 First, practice playing a polka pattern on the primary chords below.

Am (i)　　　　　Dm (iv)　　　　　Em (v)　　　　　F (VI)

2 Using any combination of notes from the A minor five-finger scale, practice improvising a melody to match the provided rhythm as you play the left-hand chord progression below.

GRAVITY
A POP PATTERN STUDY

Let's try again! As you play this piece, use any combination of notes from the
A minor five-finger scale to improvise a melody that matches the provided rhythm.

G MAJOR
G MAJOR

It's time to power up your piano skills in the key of G major with pop-infused scale practice, lead sheet triad training, chord crunching, and left-hand pattern improv. **Let's get started!**

G MAJOR MAP

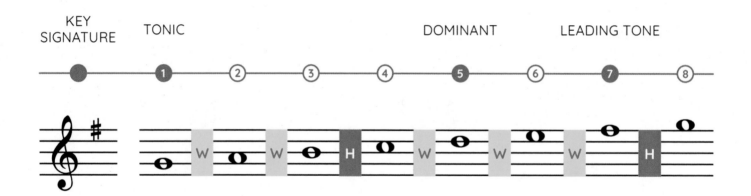

| KEY SIGNATURE | TONIC | | | | DOMINANT | | LEADING TONE | |

POP PIANO CHORDS

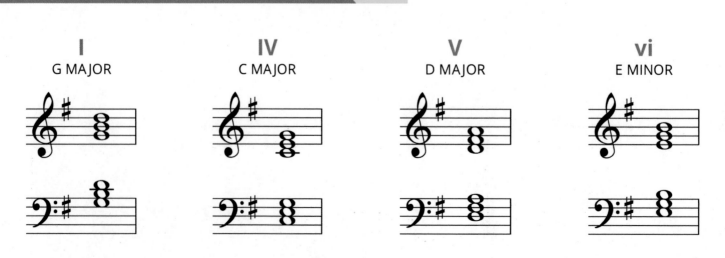

I	IV	V	vi
G MAJOR	C MAJOR	D MAJOR	E MINOR

G MAJOR SCALE PRACTICE

G MAJOR SCALE

Practice playing a two-octave G major scale using the fingering patterns on the keyboard images and the notes on the grand staff.

LH Pattern

RH Pattern

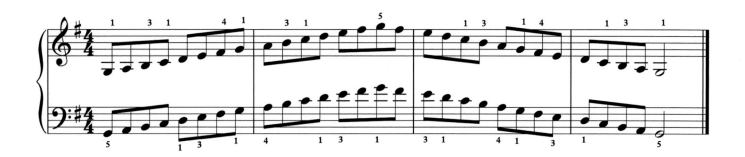

CONTRARY MOTION

Practice playing a two-octave G major scale in contrary motion. When you are ready, play the scale-focused pop piano piece on the following page.

NIGHTFALL
A G MAJOR SCALE STUDY

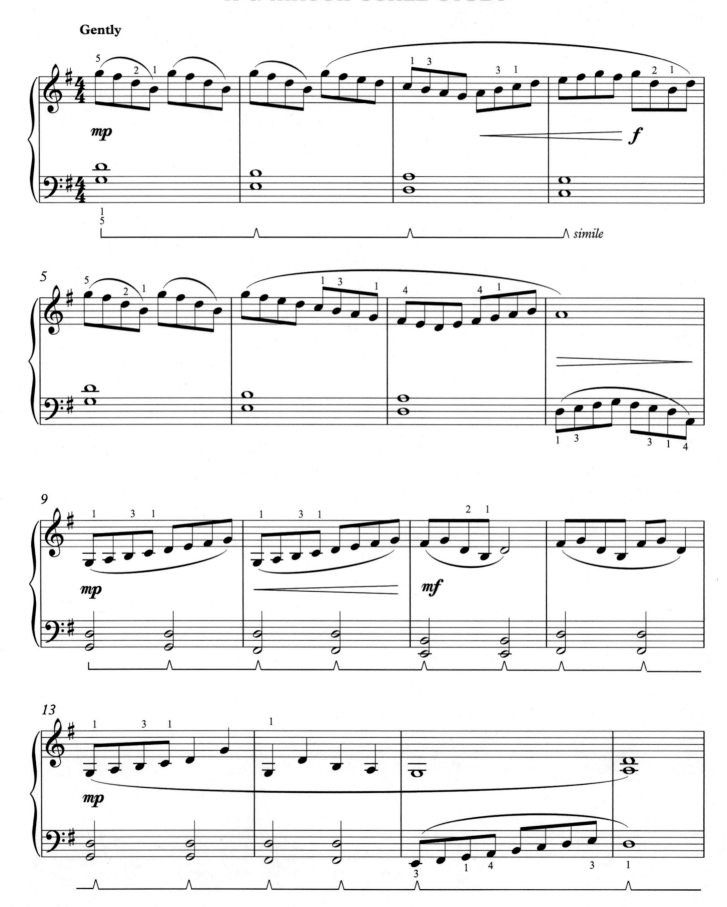

NIGHTFALL
A G MAJOR SCALE STUDY

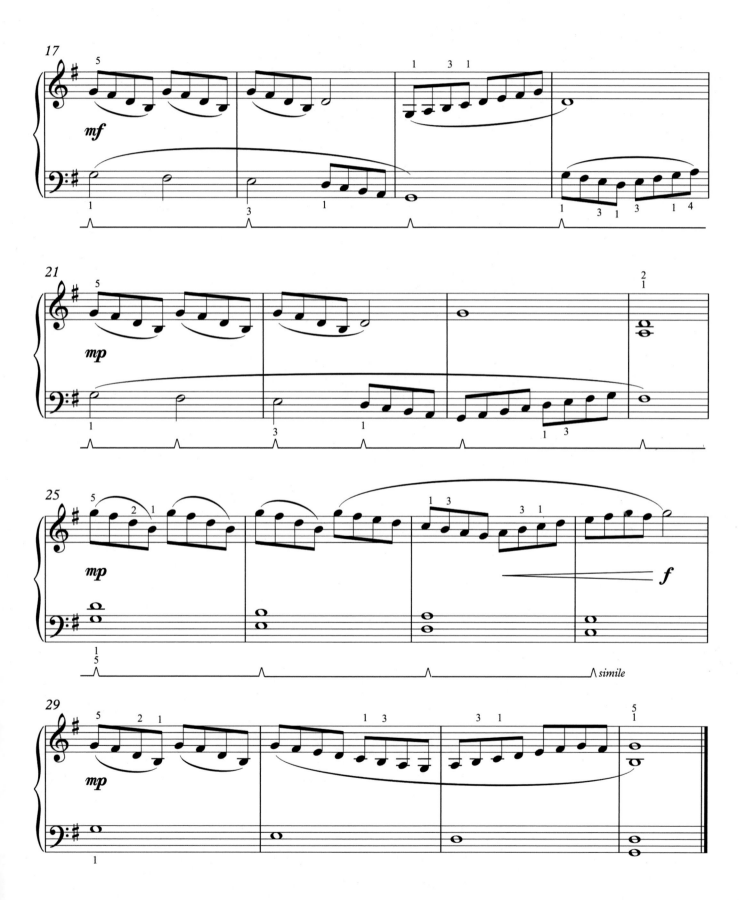

LEAD SHEET
TRIAD TRAINING

Let's put some pop in your triad training with lead sheets. **A lead sheet** uses chord symbols above the treble staff in place of the bass staff. Chord symbols dictate which chords your left hand plays while accompanying your right hand.

LET'S GET STARTED

1 The G major triad consists of the I chord (root) and its first and second inversions. Let's practice playing the triad of G major. We'll begin with a solid triad.

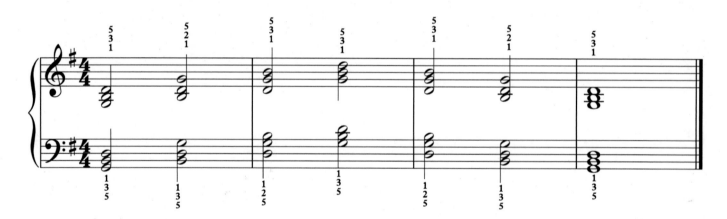

▶ Now let's practice playing the broken triad of G major. When playing a broken triad your tone should be smooth and even. Be careful not to accent the first note of each broken inversion.

2 Next, let's learn how to play from a lead sheet. A lead sheet looks like this:

When practicing the line of music above, you can play the chords as held fifths, like this:

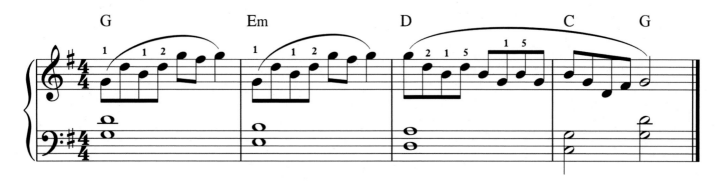

3 Finally, play the lead sheet below to rock the G major triad.

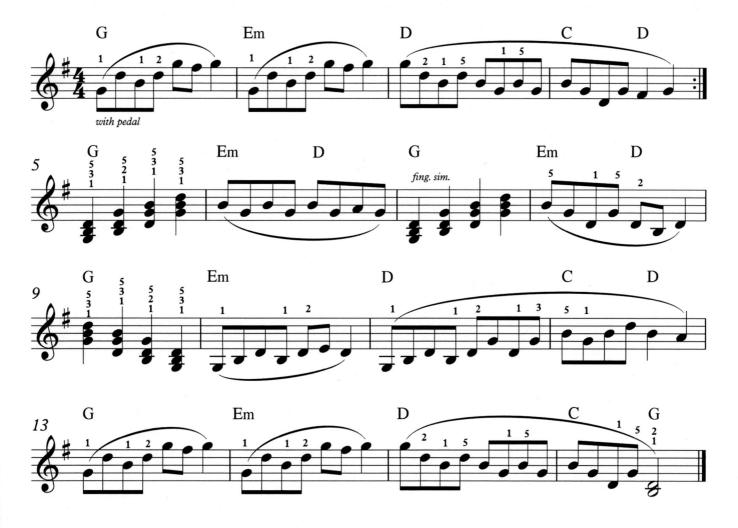

SIGHT READING
POP PIANO CHORDS

Look at the **primary chords** of G major in the measures of music below. Can you find a I chord? Can you find a IV chord? Can you find a V chord? Can you find a vi chord?

PICK A PATH

Beginning at the purple box and ending at the yellow box, play the four measures of music that rest on the dotted path. Next, I will use a colored crayon to draw a new four-measure path that begins at the purple box and ends at the yellow box. Try playing along the new path. **Let's play again.**

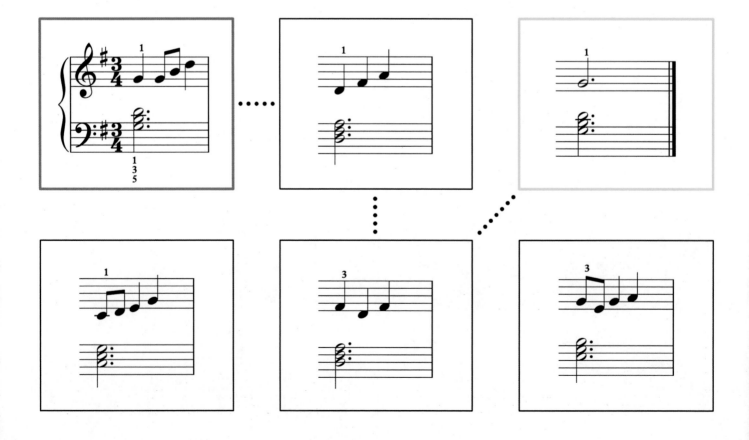

RHYTHM ROCK
POP PIANO CHORDS

Let's reinforce the primary chords of G major with a Lap Tap Clap Rhythm Duet. First, practice the body percussion above the grand staff below. Stem-down notes are performed by tapping both hands on your lap. Stem-up notes are performed by clapping your hands together. X note heads are performed by tapping your knuckles on a hard surface. Next, I will play the music as an accompaniment while you perform the body percussion. Finally, let's switch roles.

LAP TAP CLAP DUET

POP IMPROV
LEFT-HAND PATTERNS

Let's combine **left-hand patterns** with improvisation to create a pop-worthy piano experience. To begin, practice the left-hand pattern below on each of the primary chords of G major. Then, when you are ready, use any combination of notes from the G major five-finger scale to show off your improv skills on the piece that follows this page.

LET'S GET STARTED

1 First, practice playing the broken chord pattern on the primary chords below.

G (I)   **C (IV)**   **D (V)**   **Em (vi)**

2 Using any combination of notes from the G major five-finger scale, practice improvising a melody to match the provided rhythm as you play the left-hand chord progression below.

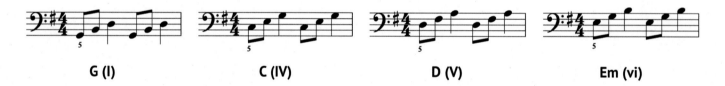

DISTANCE
A POP PATTERN STUDY

Let's try again! As you play this piece, use any combination of notes from the
G major five-finger scale to improvise a melody that matches the provided rhythm.

E MINOR
E MINOR

It's time to power up your piano skills in the key of E minor with pop-infused scale practice, lead sheet triad training, chord crunching, and left-hand pattern improv. **Let's get started!**

E MINOR MAP

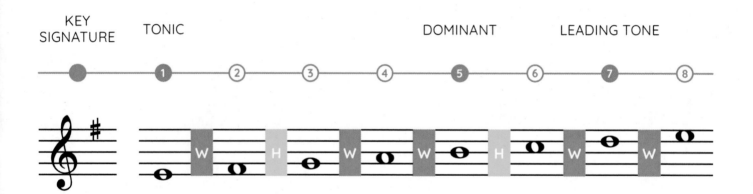

KEY SIGNATURE	TONIC				DOMINANT		LEADING TONE	
	1	2	3	4	5	6	7	8

POP PIANO CHORDS

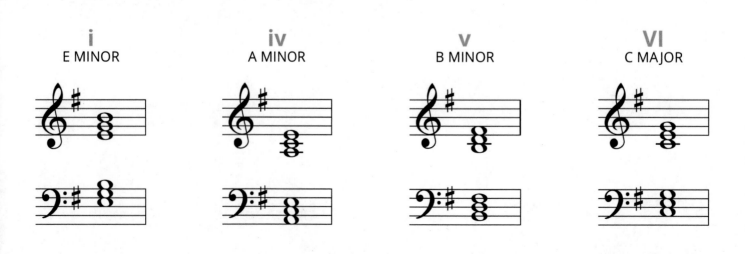

i	**iv**	**v**	**VI**
E MINOR	A MINOR	B MINOR	C MAJOR

E MINOR SCALE PRACTICE

Practice playing a two-octave E natural minor scale using the fingering patterns on the keyboard images and the notes on the grand staff.

LH Pattern

RH Pattern

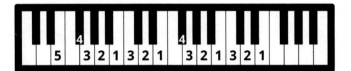

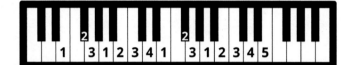

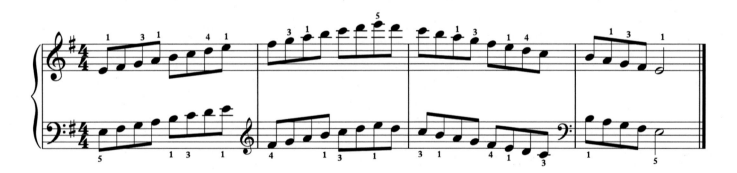

When playing the E harmonic minor scale, the leading tone (7th) is raised a half step. This is indicated by the colored notes on the staff below. Practice playing the scale.

UPRISING
AN E MINOR SCALE STUDY

Dramatically

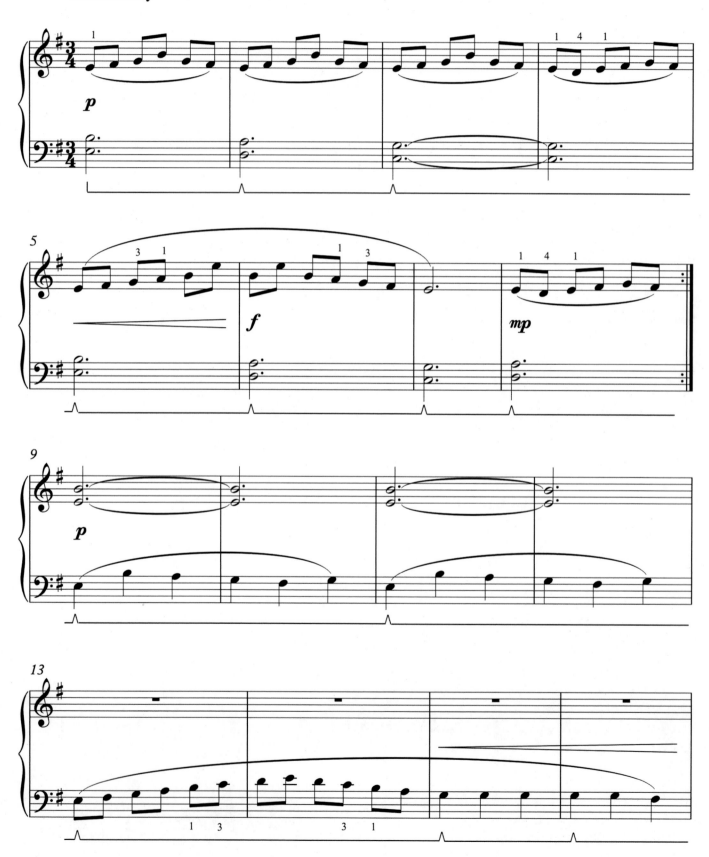

UPRISING
AN E MINOR SCALE STUDY

LEAD SHEET
TRIAD TRAINING

Let's put some pop in your triad training with lead sheets. **A lead sheet** uses chord symbols above the treble staff in place of the bass staff. Chord symbols dictate which chords your left hand plays while accompanying your right hand.

LET'S GET STARTED

1. The E minor triad consists of the i chord (root) and its first and second inversions. Let's practice playing the triad of E minor. We'll begin with a solid triad.

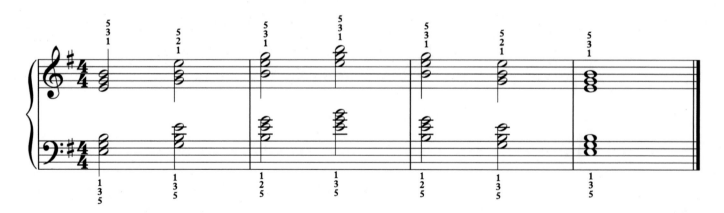

Now let's practice playing the broken triad of E minor. When playing a broken triad your tone should be smooth and even. Be careful not to accent the first note of each broken inversion.

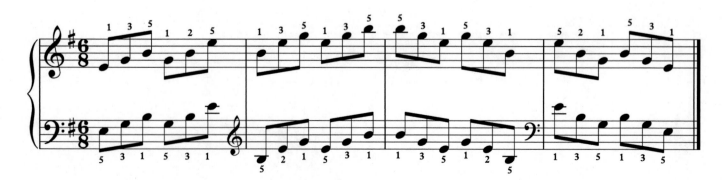

② Next, let's learn how to play from a lead sheet. A lead sheet looks like this:

▶ When practicing the line of music above, you can play the chords as held fifths, like this:

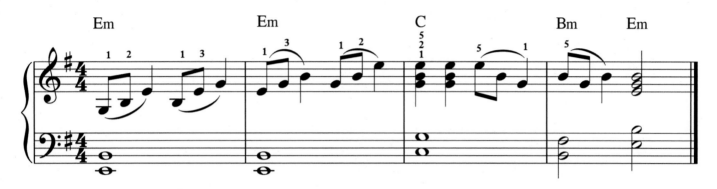

③ Finally, play the lead sheet below to rock the E minor triad.

SIGHT READING
POP PIANO CHORDS

Look at the **primary chords** of E minor in the measures of music below. Can you find a i chord? Can you find a iv chord? Can you find a v chord? Can you find a VI chord?

PICK A PATH

Beginning at the red box and ending at the yellow box, play the four measures of music that rest on the dotted path. Next, I will use a colored crayon to draw a new four-measure path that begins at the red box and ends at the yellow box. Try playing along the new path. Let's play again.

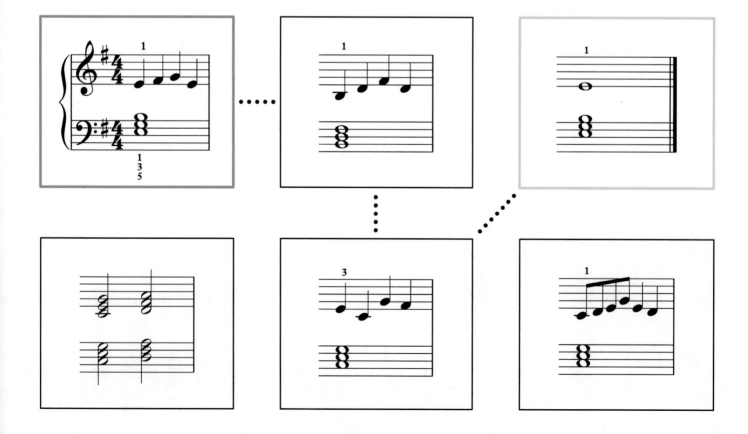

RHYTHM ROCK
POP PIANO CHORDS

Let's reinforce the primary chords of E minor with a Lap Tap Clap Rhythm Duet. First, practice the body percussion above the grand staff below. Stem-down notes are performed by tapping both hands on your lap. Stem-up notes are performed by clapping your hands together. X note heads are performed by tapping your knuckles on a hard surface. Next, I will play the music as an accompaniment while you perform the body percussion. Finally, let's switch roles.

LAP TAP CLAP DUET

POP IMPROV
LEFT-HAND PATTERNS

Let's combine **left-hand patterns** with improvisation to create a pop-worthy piano experience. To begin, practice the left-hand pattern below on each of the primary chords of E minor. Then, when you are ready, use any combination of notes from the E minor five-finger scale to show off your improv skills on the piece that follows this page.

LET'S GET STARTED

1. First, practice playing the waltz pattern on the primary chords below.

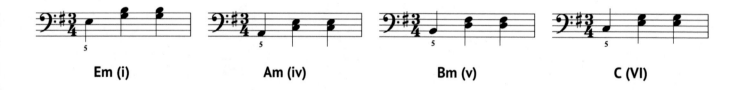

Em (i) **Am (iv)** **Bm (v)** **C (VI)**

2. Using any combination of notes from the E minor five-finger scale, practice improvising a melody to match the provided rhythm as you play the left-hand chord progression below.

mp

with pedal

CLOCKWORK
A POP PATTERN STUDY

Let's try again! As you play this piece, use any combination of notes from the
E minor five-finger scale to improvise a melody that matches the provided rhythm.

F MAJOR
F MAJOR

It's time to power up your piano skills in the key of F major with pop-infused scale practice, lead sheet triad training, chord crunching, and left-hand pattern improv. **Let's get started!**

F MAJOR MAP

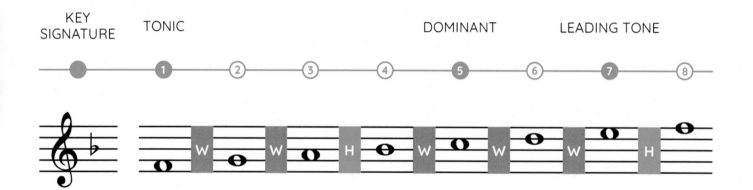

KEY SIGNATURE	TONIC				DOMINANT		LEADING TONE	

POP PIANO CHORDS

I	IV	V	vi
F MAJOR	Bb MAJOR	C MAJOR	D MINOR

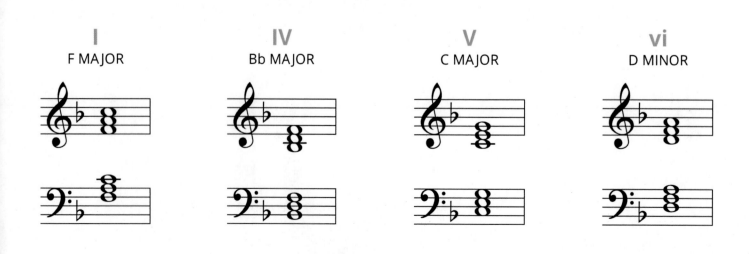

F MAJOR SCALE PRACTICE

F MAJOR SCALE

Practice playing a two-octave F major scale using the fingering patterns on the keyboard images and the notes on the grand staff.

LH Pattern

RH Pattern

CONTRARY MOTION

Practice playing a two-octave F major scale in contrary motion. When you are ready, play the scale-focused pop piano piece on the following page.

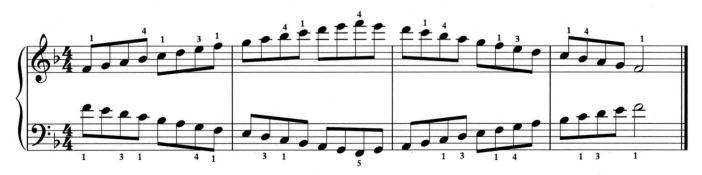

NOVEMBER
AN F MAJOR SCALE STUDY

Cheerfully

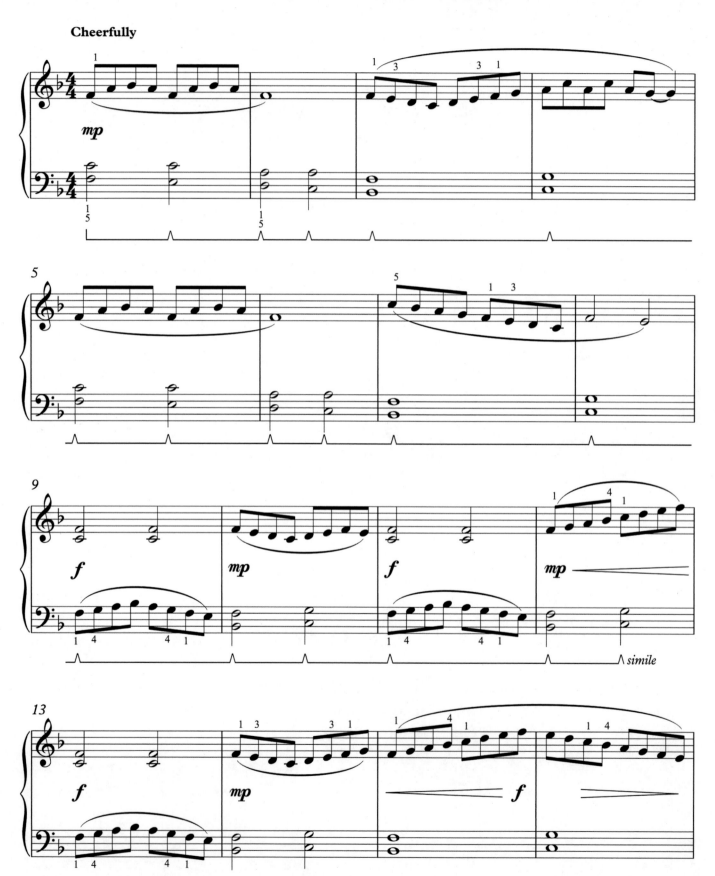

NOVEMBER
AN F MAJOR SCALE STUDY

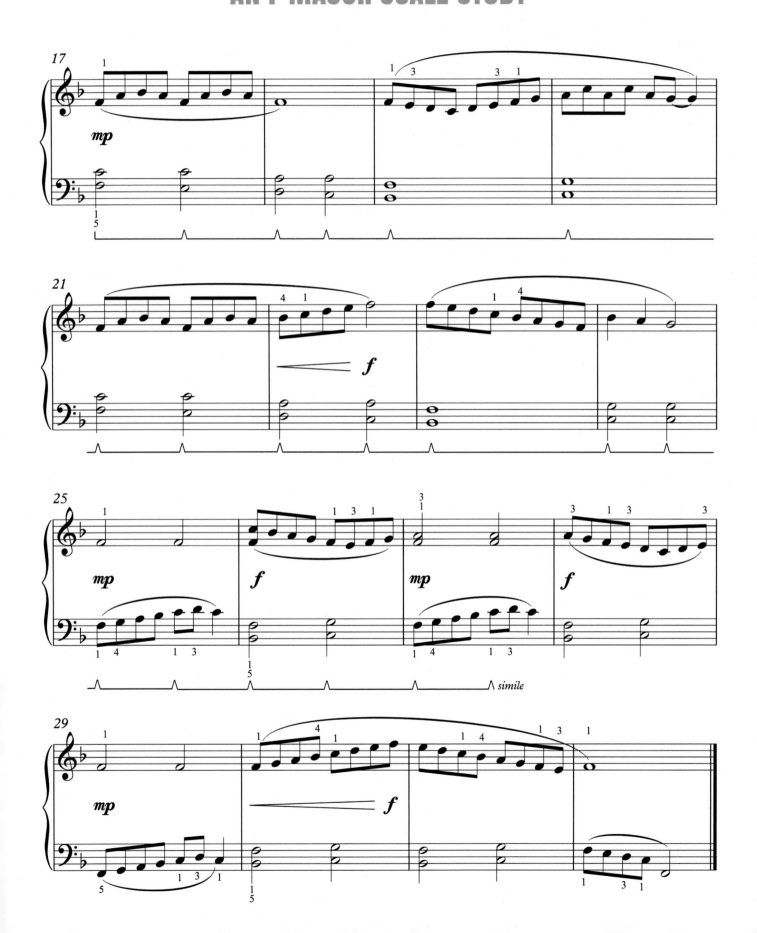

LEAD SHEET
TRIAD TRAINING

Let's put some pop in your triad training with lead sheets. **A lead sheet** uses chord symbols above the treble staff in place of the bass staff. Chord symbols dictate which chords your left hand plays while accompanying your right hand.

LET'S GET STARTED

1 The F major triad consists of the I chord (root) and its first and second inversions. Let's practice playing the triad of F major. We'll begin with a solid triad.

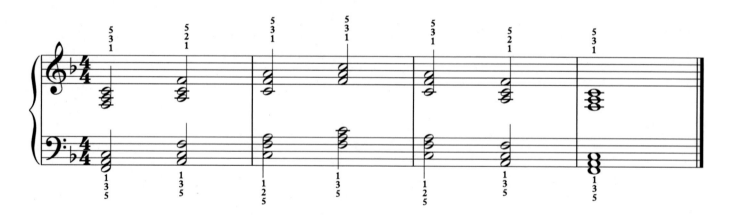

▶ Now let's practice playing the broken triad of F major. When playing a broken triad your tone should be smooth and even. Be careful not to accent the first note of each broken inversion.

2 Next, let's learn how to play from a lead sheet. A lead sheet looks like this:

▶ When practicing the line of music above, you can play the chords as held fifths, like this:

3 Finally, play the lead sheet below to rock the F major triad.

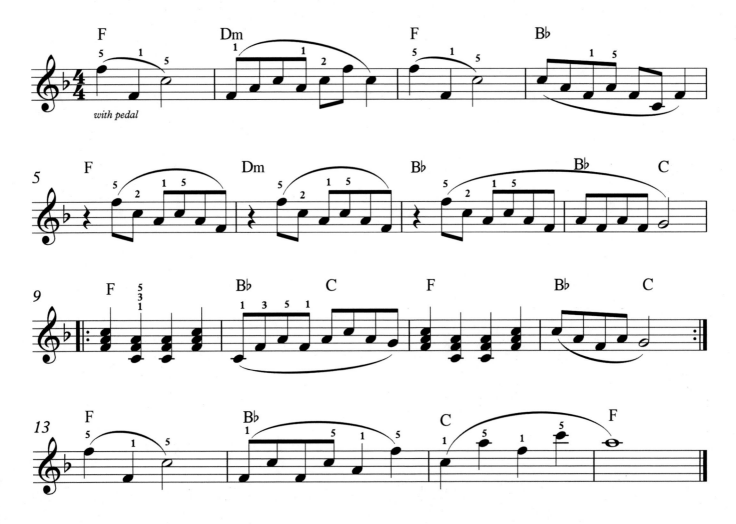

SIGHT READING
POP PIANO CHORDS

Look at the **primary chords** of F major in the measures of music below. Can you find a I chord? Can you find a IV chord? Can you find a V chord? Can you find a vi chord?

PICK A PATH

Beginning at the blue box and ending at the red box, play the four measures of music that rest on the dotted path. Next, I will use a colored crayon to draw a new four-measure path that begins at the blue box and ends at the red box. Try playing along the new path. **Let's play again.**

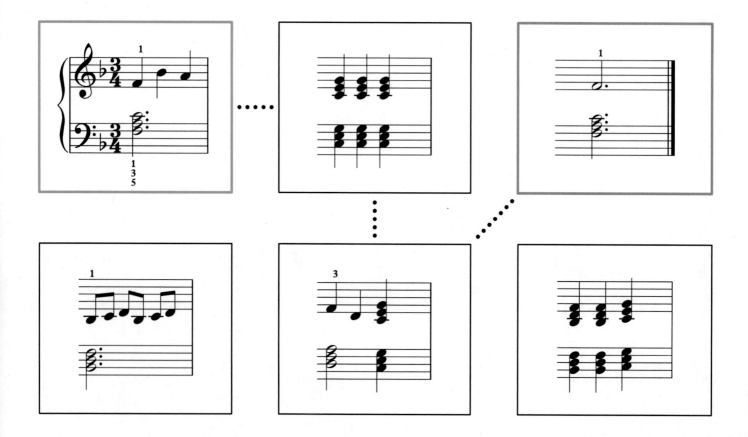

RHYTHM ROCK
POP PIANO CHORDS

Let's reinforce the primary chords of F major with a Lap Tap Clap Rhythm Duet. First, practice the body percussion above the grand staff below. Stem-down notes are performed by tapping both hands on your lap. Stem-up notes are performed by clapping your hands together. X note heads are performed by tapping your knuckles on a hard surface. Next, I will play the music as an accompaniment while you perform the body percussion. Finally, let's switch roles.

LAP TAP CLAP DUET

POP IMPROV
LEFT-HAND PATTERNS

Let's combine **left-hand patterns** with improvisation to create a pop-worthy piano experience. To begin, practice the left-hand pattern below on each of the primary chords of F major. Then, when you are ready, use any combination of notes from the F major five-finger scale to show off your improv skills on the piece that follows this page.

LET'S GET STARTED

1 First, practice playing the alberti bass pattern on the primary chords below.

F (I)   Bb (IV)   C (V)   Dm (vi)

2 Using any combination of notes from the F major five-finger scale, practice improvising a melody to match the provided rhythm as you play the left-hand chord progression below.

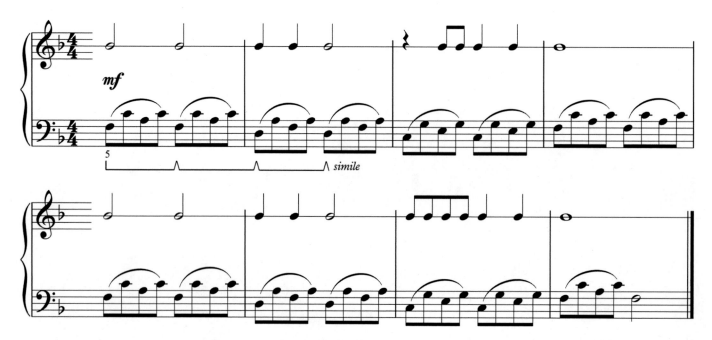

MESSENGER
A POP PATTERN STUDY

Let's try again! As you play this piece, use any combination of notes from the
F major five-finger scale to improvise a melody that matches the provided rhythm.

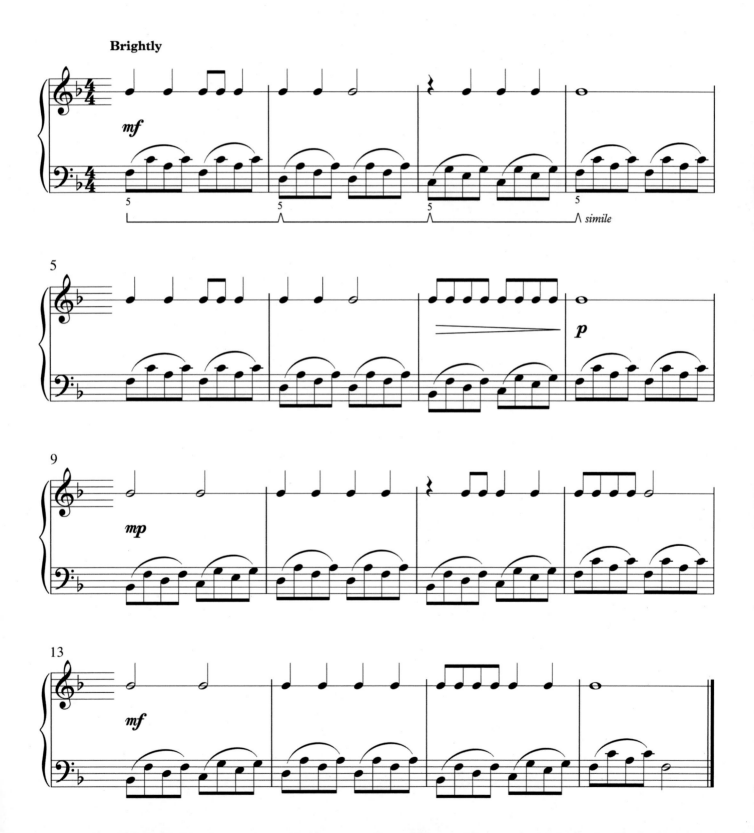

D MINOR
D MINOR

It's time to power up your piano skills in the key of D minor with pop-infused scale practice, lead sheet triad training, chord crunching, and left-hand pattern improv. **Let's get started!**

D MINOR MAP

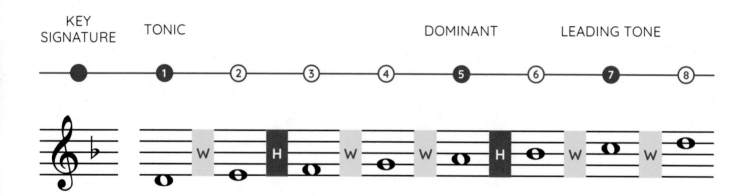

| KEY SIGNATURE | TONIC | | | | DOMINANT | | LEADING TONE | |

POP PIANO CHORDS

i
D MINOR

iv
G MINOR

v
A MINOR

VI
Bb MAJOR

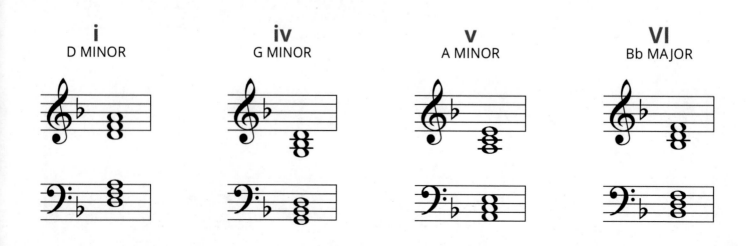

D MINOR SCALE PRACTICE

Practice playing a two-octave D natural minor scale using the fingering patterns on the keyboard images and the notes on the grand staff.

LH Pattern

RH Pattern

D HARMONIC MINOR SCALE

When playing the D harmonic minor scale, the leading tone (7th) is raised a half step. This is indicated by the colored notes on the staff below. Practice playing the scale.

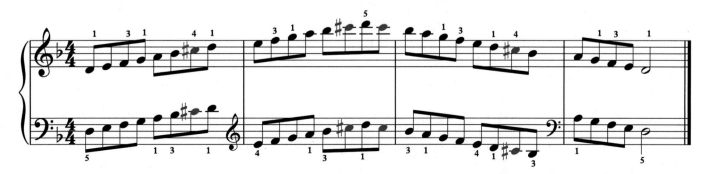

WHISPERS
A D MINOR SCALE STUDY

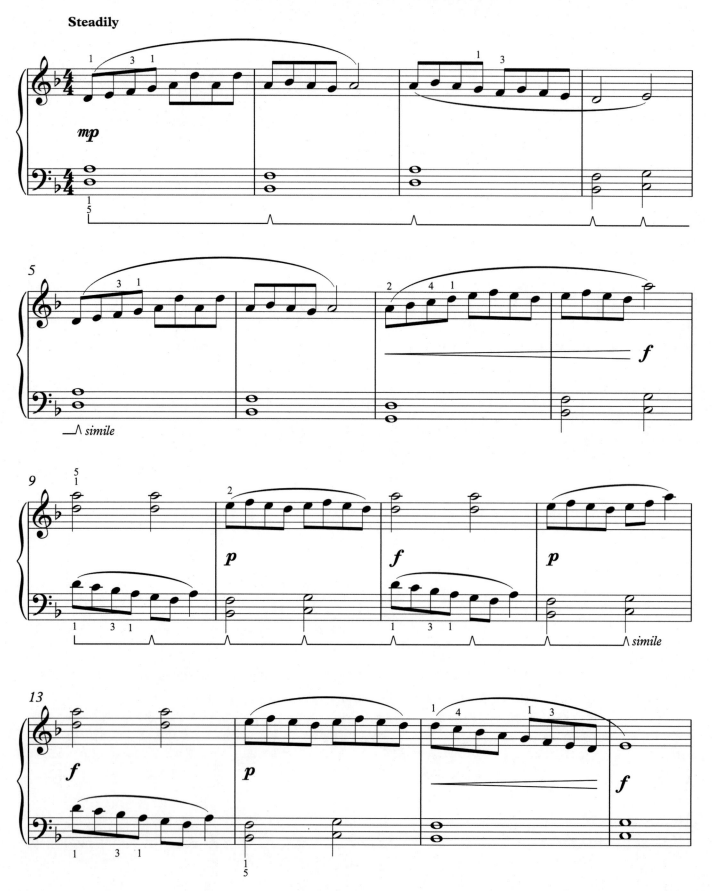

WHISPERS
A D MINOR SCALE STUDY

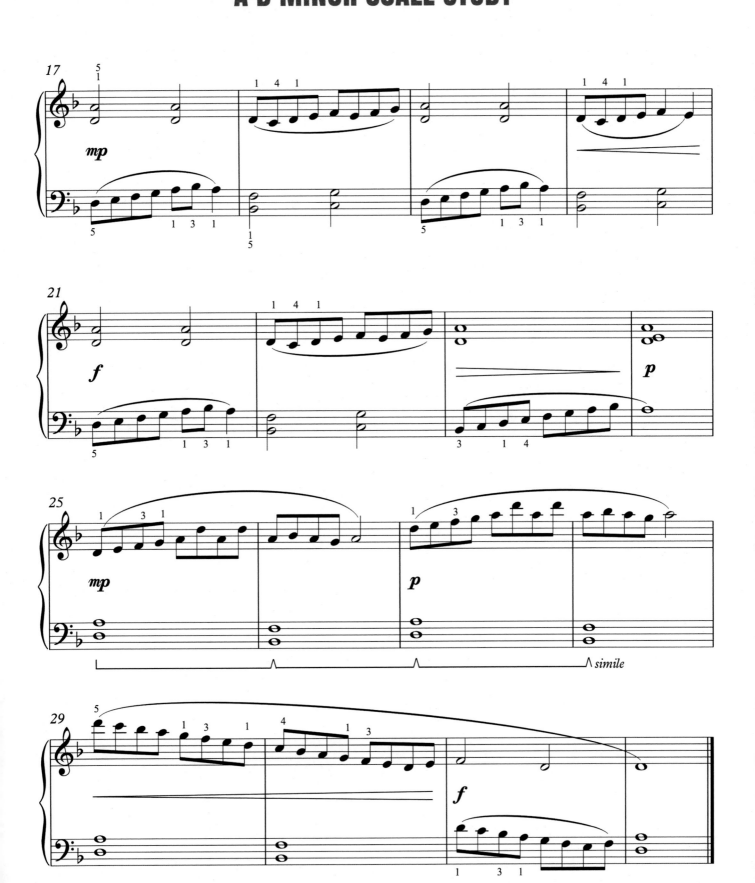

LEAD SHEET
TRIAD TRAINING

Let's put some pop in your triad training with lead sheets. **A lead sheet** uses chord symbols above the treble staff in place of the bass staff. Chord symbols dictate which chords your left hand plays while accompanying your right hand.

LET'S GET STARTED

1 The D minor triad consists of the i chord (root) and its first and second inversions. Let's practice playing the triad of D minor. We'll begin with a solid triad.

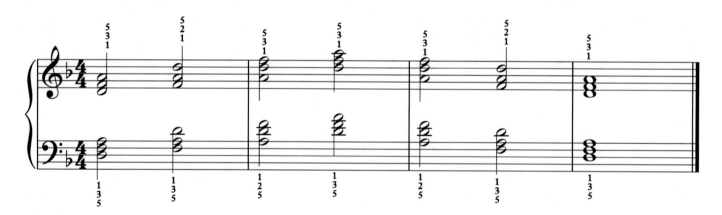

▶ Now let's practice playing the broken triad of D minor. When playing a broken triad your tone should be smooth and even. Be careful not to accent the first note of each broken inversion.

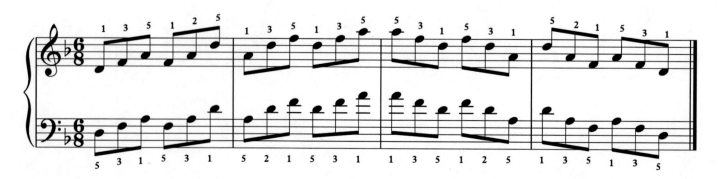

② Next, let's learn how to play from a lead sheet. A lead sheet looks like this:

▶ When practicing the line of music above, you can play the chords as held fifths, like this:

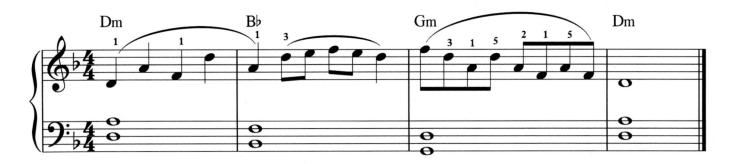

③ Finally, play the lead sheet below to rock the D minor triad.

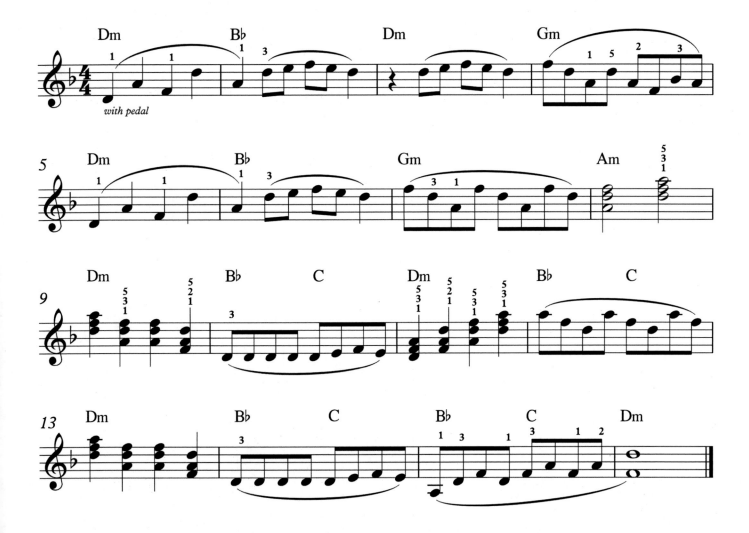

SIGHT READING
POP PIANO CHORDS

Look at the **primary chords** of D minor in the measures of music below. Can you find a i chord? Can you find a iv chord? Can you find a v chord? Can you find a VI chord?

PICK A PATH

Beginning at the purple box and ending at the yellow box, play the four measures of music that rest on the dotted path. Next, I will use a colored crayon to draw a new four-measure path that begins at the purple box and ends at the yellow box. Try playing along the new path. **Let's play again.**

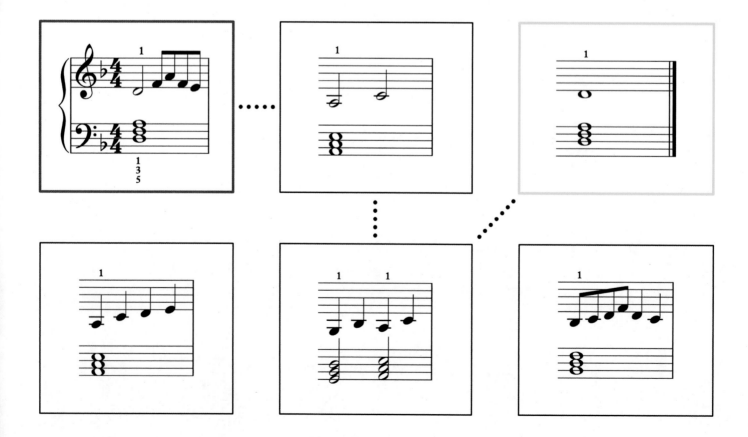

RHYTHM ROCK
POP PIANO CHORDS

Let's reinforce the primary chords of D minor with a Lap Tap Clap Rhythm Duet. First, practice the body percussion above the grand staff below. Stem-down notes are performed by tapping both hands on your lap. Stem-up notes are performed by clapping your hands together. X note heads are performed by tapping your knuckles on a hard surface. Next, I will play the music as an accompaniment while you perform the body percussion. Finally, let's switch roles.

LAP TAP CLAP DUET

POP IMPROV
LEFT-HAND PATTERNS

Let's combine **left-hand patterns** with improvisation to create a pop-worthy piano experience. To begin, practice the left-hand pattern below on each of the primary chords of D minor. Then, when you are ready, use any combination of notes from the D minor five-finger scale to show off your improv skills on the piece that follows this page.

LET'S GET STARTED

1 First, practice playing the broken chord pattern on the primary chords below.

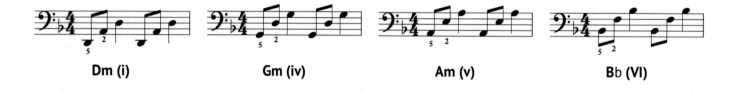

Dm (i)   **Gm (iv)**   **Am (v)**   **Bb (VI)**

2 Using any combination of notes from the D minor five-finger scale, practice improvising a melody to match the provided rhythm as you play the left-hand chord progression below.